Egg Cozies

GUILD OF MASTER CRAFTSMAN PUBLICATIONS

First published 2010 by
Guild of Master Craftsman Publications Ltd
Castle Place, 166 High Street,
Lewes, East Sussex BN7 1XU

ISBN 978-1-86108-684-6

Charts and pattern checking by Gina Alton

Associate Publisher: Jonathan Bailey
Production Manager: Jim Bulley
Managing Editor: Gerrie Purcell
Senior Project Editor: Virginia Brehaut
Managing Art Editor: Gilda Pacitti
Design: Ali Walper
Photographer: Laurel Guilfoyle

Set in Gill Sans

Colour origination by GMC Reprographics
Printed and bound in Thailand by KNP

Why we love egg cozies

THERE IS NOTHING QUITE LIKE WAKING up to a cooked breakfast or brunch on a cold morning, and what could be better than a comforting boiled egg and toast. Popular the world over, eggs are a delicious and nutritious meal and provide a great start to any day. These gorgeous egg cozies will keep your eggs warm and toasty (no pun intended). They're easy, fun and quick to make, ideal for the breakfast table or as small gifts for friends and family. Created in a wide range of styles, there's something to suit everyone's taste and humour.

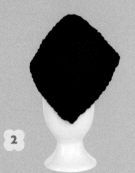

1

2

3

4

Contents

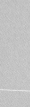

5

6

7

8

9

10

11

12

13

14

15

16

17   **18**   **19**   **20**

21   **22**   **23**   **24**

25

26

27

28

29

30

Clair Thorley's jaunty jester's hat egg cozy is fun, bright and will keep the jokes flowing over the breakfast table. The bells at the top of each point make the perfect finishing touch.

Only yolking

Materials

Any 4-ply merino wool yarns in red, green and blue (2 small balls in each colour for the intarsia section)

A pair of 3.25mm (UK10:US3) needles

6 x small gold bells

Sewing needle and thread

Darning needle

Tension

28 sts and 36 rows to 4in (10cm) over st st using 3.25mm needles. Use larger or smaller needles to obtain correct tension.

Pattern notes

At each 'm1', twist the loop to prevent a hole from forming.

Method

This jester hat cozy is knitted in rows from the bottom up, starting with a stripy 2 × 2 rib and then working in stocking stitch intarsia in 6 columns of colour. Stitches are increased to shape the points at the top, each point finished individually and then stitches are decreased to make a point at the tip. Finally the side seam is sewn as well as the seams on each point, and a little bell is stitched to each of the six tips.

Hat

With 3.25mm needles and blue, cast on 42 sts.

In 2 × 2 rib, work 2 rows in blue, 2 rows in red and then 2 rows in green.

Row 1: (K7 in green, k7 in blue, k7 in red) twice.

Row 2: (P7 in red, p7 in blue, p7 in green) twice.

Rows 3–14: Rep rows 1–2 six times.

Row 15: *(K1, m1, k5, m1, k1) in green, (k1, m1, k5, m1, k1) in blue, (k1, m1, k5, m1, k1) in red, rep from * once (54 sts).

Row 16: *(P1, m1, p7, m1, p1) in red, (p1, m1, p7, m1, p1) in blue, (p1, m1, p7, m1, p1) in green, rep from * once (66 sts).

Row 17: *(K1, m1, k9, m1, k1) in green, (k1, m1, k9, m1, k1) in blue, (k1, m1, k9, m1, k1) in red, rep from * once (78 sts).

Row 18: *(P1, m1, p11, m1, p1) in red, (p1, m1, p11, m1, p1) in blue, (p1, m1, p11, m1, p1) in green, rep from * once (90 sts).

Row 19: *(K1, m1, k13, m1, k1) in green, (k1, m1, k13, m1, k1) in blue, (k1, m1, k13, m1, k1) in red, rep from * once (102 sts).

Row 20: *(P1, m1, p15, m1, p1) in red, (p1, m1, p15, m1, p1) in blue, (p1, m1, p15, m1, p1) in green, rep from * once (114 sts). 19 sts per colour section.

Rows 21–22: Work even in st st, keeping colour changes correct.

**Row 23: (K1, k2tbl, k13, k2tog, k1) in green, turn. 17 sts in this green colour section.

Cont to work in green on these sts only, as folls:

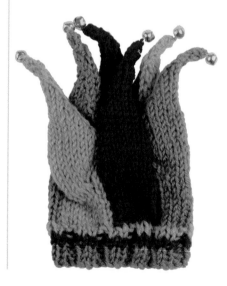

Row 24: P1, p2tog, p11, p2tog, p1, turn (15 sts).

Row 25: K1, k2tbl, k9, k2tog, k1, turn (13 sts).

Row 26: Purl.

Row 27: K1, k2tbl, k7, k2tog, k1, turn (11 sts).

Row 28: Purl.

Row 29: K1, k2tbl, k5, k2tog, k1, turn (9 sts).

Row 30: Purl.

Row 31: K1, k2tbl, k3, k2tog, k1, turn (7 sts).

Row 32: Purl.

Row 33: K1, k2tbl, k1, k2tog, k1, turn (5 sts).

Row 34: Purl.

Next row: K1, (sl1, k2tog, psso), k1.

Next row: Purl.

Next row: K3tog.

Fasten off.**

Rep from ** to ** for the other 5 pointed sections of the hat, in the appropriate colours.

Making up

With a darning needle, join the side seam. Then sew seams loosely down from each point of the hat and secure the point in the middle where they all meet. With sewing needle and thread, sew a bell to the end of each of the points.

This pair of 'his and hers' cozies by Gina Alton brings a special touch to an intimate breakfast for two. Blue for him, pink for her and a love heart each for adornment.

Sweethearts

Materials

Any DK yarns in pink, blue and red
A pair of 4mm (UK8:US6) needles
A 3.5mm (UK9:USE/4) crochet hook
Darning needle

Tension

Not critical as fabric is very stretchy

Method

These matching cozies are made in garter stitch. Two squares are joined together along two adjacent sides to form the base. The heart motif is made separately and also in garter stitch. Cast on and work downwards for the lower half, then pick up and knit upwards for the two crescents at the top. The border is neatened with a round of crocheted slip stitch and the heart then stitched on as appliqué.

Back

With 4mm needles and pink or blue yarn, cast on 14 sts.
Work 25 rows even in garter stitch (or until piece is square).
Cast off loosely and break off yarn.

Front

Make a second piece as for back, but do not break off yarn.
Place pieces tog and ss to join two adjacent sides of the squares, leaving the other two sides unstitched for the opening of the cozy.

Heart

Lower half (worked from the centre downwards)
With 4mm needles and red yarn, cast on 10 sts and work 2 rows even in g-st.
Row 1 (RS): Knit.
Row 2: Knit.
Next: Cont to work in g-st, dec 1 st at beg of each foll row until 0 sts rem. Break off yarn.

Upper half (worked from the centre upwards)
Turn lower half of heart upside-down so cast-on edge is at the top and RS facing.
Right-hand crescent
Row 1: Now pick up and k the first 5 sts beg at the RH edge, turn.
Row 2: K these 5 sts.
Row 3: K2tog, k3 (4 sts).
Row 4: K2tog, k2 (3 sts).
Cast off k-wise and break off yarn.
Left-hand crescent
Pick up and k the rem 5 sts along cast-on edge and work as for RH crescent, but do not break off yarn.
With 3.5mm hook, ss all around perimeter of heart to neaten the edge.

Making up

With darning needle and red yarn, stitch heart onto cozy centre front and darn in ends.

This pretty basket of violets by Charmaine Fletcher will add a touch of country charm to the breakfast table. Each delicate violet is finished off with a gold bead in the centre.

Purple haze

Materials

Any DK yarns in beige, jade green and purple

11 gold beads

A pair each 3mm (UK11:US2–3)

and 4mm (UK8:US6) needles

A set of 4mm (UK8:US6) double-pointed needles

Sewing needle

Tapestry needle

Invisible sewing thread

Tape measure

Dressmaker's pins

Tension

Not critical

Pattern notes

This cozy is designed to accommodate most egg cups but works particularly well on stemmed designs.

Special abbreviations

Skpo: slip one stitch, knit one stitch, then pass the slipped stitch over.

Purple haze basket chart *36 sts x 14 rows*

Each square = 1 st and 1 row

Knit

Knit

Purl

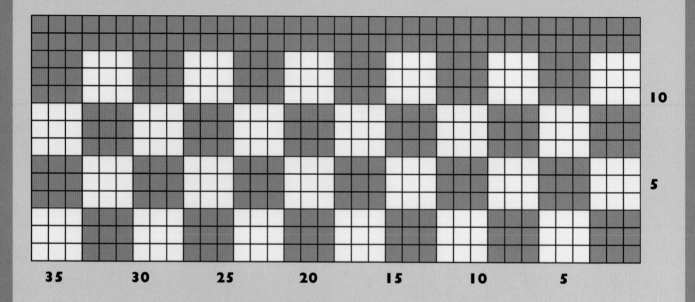

10

5

35   30   25   20   15   10   5

Method

The basket is knitted first, from the bottom upwards in rounds and a basket weave-style pattern. After 14 rows the chart work is complete and the colour changed to green for the grass, worked in stocking stitch and decreasing for closure at the top. An I-cord handle is added to the basket; then purple flowers are made and added on, with a single gold bead in the centre of each.

Basket

With 4mm DPNs and beige, cast on 36 sts and arrange over 3 needles. Working in rounds, follow the chart from beg to end to form the basket. Change to green yarn.

Rounds 1–9: Knit.

Round 10: (K7, skpo) to end (32 sts).

Round 11: (K6, skpo) to end (28 sts).

Round 12: (K5, skpo) to end (24 sts).

Round 13: (K4, skpo) to end (20 sts).

Round 14: (K3, skpo) to end (16 sts).

Round 15: (K2, skpo) to end (12 sts).

Round 16: (K1, skpo) to end (8 sts).

Break off yarn, leaving tail for sewing and thread end through rem sts to close.

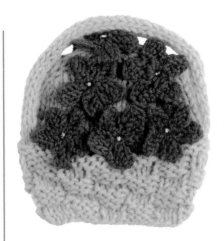

Handle

With 4mm DPNs and beige yarn cast on 4 sts, leaving a 4in (10cm) tail at the beg for sewing later.

Make an I-cord tube approx 10in (25cm) long by knitting all rows from right to left, sliding the sts back to the RH end of the needle to start each new row and pulling the yarn tightly behind the work between rows.

Fasten off, leaving a tail for sewing and draw end through sts to close.

Sew onto the basket by pulling ends through to the WS and securing the last ½in (1.5cm) of each end with stitching.

Violets

(make 11, or more if preferred)

With 3mm needles and purple yarn, cast on 5 sts.

Rows 1–2: K5, turn.

Row 3: Cast off 3 sts, (loop left on needle counts as 1 stitch), k1, turn (2 sts rem).

First petal complete.

Row 4: K2, cast on 3 sts, turn (5 sts).

Rows 5–6: K5, turn.

Row 7: Cast off 3 sts, (loop left on needle counts as 1 stitch), k1, turn (2 sts rem).

Second petal complete.

Rep rows 4–7 three times (for third, fourth and fifth petals).

Fasten off, leaving a tail for sewing.

Optional leaves

(see tip on page 23)

With 3mm needles and green, cast on 3 sts.

Row 1: Knit.

Row 2: Purl.

Row 3: K1, m1, k1, m1, k1 (5 sts).

Row 4: Purl.

Row 5: K1, m1, k3, m1, k1 (7 sts).

Row 6: Purl.

Row 7: Knit.

Row 8: Purl.

Row 9: K2tog, k3, skpo (5 sts).

Row 10: Purl.

Row 11: K2tog, k1, skpo (3 sts).

Row 12: Purl.

Row 13: K3tog.

Fasten off, using the loop to draw the thread through to a leaf-like point; then gently sew the rem tail down the LH side to the bottom. Break off yarn. Rep for as many leaves as desired, sewing on and darning in ends as you go.

Tip

You could make white flowers instead, add a few leaves and have a basket of summer daisies. Or in blue, create forget-me-not flowers. Alternatively, use up yarn-stash oddments for an abundance of colour, adding the leaves to 'blend' from one colour into the next.

Making up
Violets

There are 2 tails to each flower: 1 on top of the first petal and 1 at the base of the last petal. Using the base tail, draw it along the inner petal edges and gently pull together to form a flower. Then, working it along each petal edge, define the flower petals in turn, forming a gentle curve, catching the top tail and drawing it down to the centre, over-sewing it with the working base tail. Fasten off, but leave the top tail (now drawn down to the centre) to stitch on to the greenery. Repeat this process with the other flowers. Arrange randomly over the green area and sew on.

Add the bead centre by using invisible thread and a loop start (double over the thread, pass through the needle's eye, bringing the needle through the greenery and through the thread loop to secure without a knot). It is easier to go from flower to flower, until all the beads have been used, securing the invisible thread without cutting then trim it later. Darn in any loose ends.

Handle

Sew to the basket by pulling ends through to the WS and securing the last ½in (1.5cm) of each end with stitching.

This colourful cozy by Zee Miller is inspired by the hats worn by Rastafarians and makes the ideal accessory for fans of West Indian music. Complete the effect by adding as many dreadlocks as you like.

Reggae cup

Materials

Any DK yarns in red, yellow, green and black
3mm (UK11:USC2–D/3) crochet hook

Tension

Not critical

Method

The cozy is crocheted from the top down in rounds of stripes. The 'dreadlocks' are formed from a series of one-row pieces joined together, which are then sewn onto the top.

Cozy

Round 1: With red yarn, make a loop and work 12tr into loop. Pull loop to tighten and fasten off securely. Slip stitch to join into ring.

Round 2: (2tr into first tr, 1tr into next tr) to end (18 tr).
Join in yellow yarn.

Round 3: (2tr in first tr, 1tr in each of next 2 tr) to end (24 tr).
Join in green yarn.

Round 4: (2tr in first tr, 1tr in each of next 3 tr) to end (30 tr).
Change to red yarn.

Round 5: Work 1 tr in each tr to end. Join with ss into a ring.
Change to yellow yarn.

Round 6: Work 1tr in each tr to end. Join with ss into a ring.
Change to green yarn.

Round 7: Work 1tr in each tr to end. Join with ss into a ring.
Change to red yarn.

Round 8: Work 1dc in each tr to end. Join with ss into a ring.
Fasten off.

Dreadlocks

Using black yarn, make 25ch. Work 1dc into each chain loop, allowing work to twist for a realistic 'dreads' effect. When you reach the end, make another length of 24ch and work back along it. Continue in this way, working one fewer ch st each time until you have a bunch containing as many 'dreads' as you require. Fasten off, leaving a long end to attach bunch of dreadlocks to cozy.

Making up

Sew in ends. Pull 'dreads' through small hole at top of cozy and sew to attach securely.

This graceful ballerina by Tracey Douthwaite is the perfect gift for any little would-be dancer. She has a knitted body and crocheted arms, legs and tutu.

Ballet dancer

Materials

Any DK yarns in light pink, white and yellow

A pair of 4mm (UK8:US6) needles

4mm (UK8:USG/6) hook

Darning needle

Sewing needle

Blue and red thread for eyes and mouth

Tension

Not critical

Method

Begin by knitting the dress, from the hem upwards. The stitches decrease for the shoulders then white yarn is joined in for the head. There are some intarsia rows where the white face and yellow hair are formed, then continue in yellow only to complete the hairstyle. A band of yellow yarn secures the bun at the top of the head, and a collar in pink draws the neckline closed. Arms and legs are made with crochet chains and a single row of double crochet and attached to the body. Eyes and a mouth are embroidered. Finally, stitches are picked up around the middle and the tutu is crocheted on in the round.

Cozy

With 4mm needles and pink, cast on 24 sts.

Hem

Rows 1–4: Work in rev st st (p on RS, k on WS).

Dress

Rows 5–11: Work in st st (k on RS, p on WS).
Row 12 (WS): Knit (this creates purl loops on the RS, for crocheting the tutu later).
Rows 13–16: Work in st st.

Row 17 (RS): (P2tog) 12 times (12 sts). Change to white.

Neck

Row 18: Purl.

Head

Row 19: Knit, inc 1 st at each end of row (14 sts).
Row 20: Purl.
Join in yellow for hair.
Row 21: K5 in yellow, k4 in white, k5 in yellow.
Row 22: P5 in yellow, p4 in white, p5 in yellow.
Row 23: As row 21.
Break off white and cont in yellow only.
Row 24 (WS): Purl.
Row 25 (RS): Knit.
Rows 26–29: Rep rows 24–25 twice.
Row 30: (P2tog) 7 times (7 sts).
Row 31: (K2tog) 3 times, p1 (4 sts).
Row 32: (P2tog) twice (2 sts).
Break off yarn leaving a tail for sewing and pull end through rem sts.

Making up

With darning needle, sew seam sections (dress, head and hair). Wrap a length of yellow yarn tightly around the top of the hair and knot to make the bun. Lightly stuff the head with some white yarn. Wrap a length of pink yarn around the neck tightly and knot to secure. With sewing needle, embroider eyes in blue thread and mouth in red thread.

Legs (make 2)

With 4mm hook and pink yarn, mk 10ch.
Row 1: Sk1ch, 9dc.
Break off yarn leaving a tail for sewing. Attach to cozy inside hem.

Arms (make 2)

With 4mm hook and white yarn, mk 15ch.
Row 1: Sk1ch, 14dc.
Break off yarn leaving a tail for sewing.

Tutu

Round 1: With 4mm hook and pink yarn, pick up and work 1ch into each p st along middle of body.
Round 2: Mk 3ch, turn and work 2 trtr into each ch to end, to increase, then ss to join.
Round 3: Mk 2ch, turn and wk a dtr in between each trtr st to end, then 1ss to join rnd.
Fasten off.
Darn in any loose ends.

This tiny creation by Billie Foulk is just like the traditional tea cozies Grandma used to make, but in miniature. The cotton yarn is easy to wash, and the funky colour combination brings it right up to date.

Tiny traditional

Materials

Any 4-ply cotton yarns
Approx 20g each in bright pink (MC) and ecru (CC)
A pair of 3.25mm (UK10:US3) needles
1 small mother-of-pearl button

Tension

Not critical

Method

This cozy is knitted from bottom to top in 5-stitch columns alternating between the main colour and contrast colour. The yarn not in use is pulled tightly across the back to form pleats on the right side of the fabric. The finishing touch is a little mother-of-pearl button right at the top.

Cozy

With MC, cast on 62 sts and work 2 rows g-st. Join in CC and patt as folls, drawing yarn not in use tightly across back of work to form pleats:

Row 1 (RS): K1 in MC, (k5 in CC, k5 in MC) to last st, k1 in CC.

Row 2 (WS): K1 in CC, (k5 in MC, k5 in CC) to last st, k1 in MC.

These 2 rows form patt.

Rep patt until work measures 3½in (9cm), ending with RS facing for next row.

Shape top

Row 1: K1 in MC, *(k2tog, k1, k2tog) in CC, (k2tog, k1, k2tog) in MC; rep from * to last st, k1 in CC (38 sts).

Row 2: K1 in CC, (k3 in MC, k3 in CC) to last st, k1 in MC.

Row 3: K1 in MC, *(k2tog, k1) in CC, (k2tog, k1) in MC to last st, k1 in CC (26 sts).

Row 4: K1 in CC, (k2 in MC, k2 in CC), to last st, k1 in MC.

Row 5: K1 in MC, (k2tog in CC, k2tog in MC) to last st, k1 in CC (14 sts).

Row 6: (K1 in CC, k1 in MC) to end.

Row 7: With MC only (k2tog) to end (7 sts).

Thread yarn through rem sts. Fasten off.

Making up
To finish off

Join side seam using backstitch so contrast sts at each edge do not show. Attach button to top of cozy.

Note: if you prefer, you can make a tiny pompom to decorate the top of this cozy.

Envelop your egg in this ingenious wrap by Pollie Fenn. The clever woven finish gives it a rugged tweed-like effect, which is perfectly finished off by the smart toggle button.

Cozy wrap

Materials

Biggan Design DK Merino First Cross Pure New Wool
(105m/115yds per 50g ball)
1 x 50g ball in 630 Imperial Jade
A small amount of two other DK yarns in complementary
(contrast) colours
A pair of 4mm (UK8:US6) needles
1 wooden toggle
Darning needle

Tension

Not critical

Method

This cozy would suit a taller egg cup with a stem. It is knitted first as a rectangle in garter stitch; then one contrast colour is woven along the fabric along the 'high' points of the garter stitches and a second colour is woven along through the 'low' points of the stitches. Finally a wooden toggle (or button of your choice) is sewn on as a fastening to keep the 'cone' shape secure.

Cozy

With 4mm needles cast on 18 sts. Work 56 rows in garter stitch. Cast off loosely.

Interim finishing

Block the piece of knitting.

'Woven' finish

Either make up the cozy as it is or give it a woven look, as folls: With one of the contrast colours and starting on the left-hand side, work running stitches through the high points of the garter stitches from cast-on edge to cast-off edge.

Complete in rows across the whole piece finishing at the right-hand side. Then with the other contrast colour, work running stitches through the low points of the garter stitches between each line worked in the first contrast colour.

Making up

Pull the piece round as you would a wrap; so the knitted rows run vertical and overlap at the top. Then sew on the toggle to secure the overlap. Darn in any loose ends.

Fried egg or boiled egg? It's a hard decision, but now you can have the best of both worlds with Alexandra McKee's mouth-watering egg cozy.

Sunny side up

Materials

Any 4-ply cotton yarns in lemon and ecru
A set of four 3mm (UK11:US2–3) double-pointed needles
Tapestry needle

Tension

24 sts and 28 rows to 4in (10cm) over st st using 3mm needles. Use larger or smaller needles to obtain correct tension.

Method

The rounded piece that fits over the egg is made first in lemon, worked in the round from bottom to top. The piece is then turned around and the cast-on stitches picked up and knitted. The 'frill' effect is made by increasing stitches on two separate rounds.

Cozy

With lemon yarn, cast on 42 sts and divide between 3 DPNs. 14 sts each. Place marker at beg of round.

Rounds 1–10: Knit.

Round 11: (K9, k2tog, k8, k2tog) twice (38 sts).

Round 12: (K8, k2tog, k7, k2tog) twice (34 sts).

Round 13: (K7, k2tog, k6, k2tog) twice (30 sts).

Round 14: (K6, k2tog, k5, k2tog) twice (26 sts).

Round 15: (K5, k2tog, k4, k2tog) twice (22 sts).

Round 16: (K2tog) to end (11 sts).

Round 17: (K2tog) to last st, k1 (6 sts).

Round 18: (K2tog) to end (3 sts). Thread yarn through the 3 rem sts to tie off.

Ruffle

At base of egg cozy and with ecru, pick up and k 42 sts in the round. K 2 more rounds.

Round 4: K1, (yo, k1) to end.

Rounds 5–7: Knit (working each yo as a k st too).

Round 8: As row 4.

Rounds 9–10: Knit. Cast off k-wise.

Finishing

Darn in loose ends.

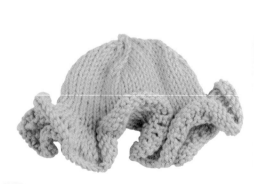

EGG COZIES

Pretty and pink, this design by Gina Alton is perfect for little princesses who like a touch of glamour in their lives. The pearly beads are in one long string and are secured at the back.

Pearly girly

Materials

Any DK yarn in dusky pink
A pair of 4mm (UK8:US6) needles
1yd (1m) string of white beads
Darning needle

Tension

Not critical

Special abbreviations

K3tog: Knit 3 sts together

Method

The cozy is knitted in rows from bottom to top in stocking stitch with just one row of garter stitch near the start and decreasing by k3togs at the top. The top is drawn closed and the side seam sewn, then the string of beads is draped around like a necklace and stitched at a point along the seam to secure.

Cozy

With 4mm needles cast on 33 sts.

Row 1 (RS): Knit.
Row 2: Purl.
Row 3: Knit.
Row 4 (g-st row): Knit.
Row 5 (RS): Knit.
Rows 6–21: Cont in st st.
Row 22 (WS): (P3tog) to end (11 sts). Leave sts on needle and break off yarn leaving a tail for sewing.

Making up

With darning needle, thread yarn through rem 11 sts, pull tight to close and secure with a knot. Sew side seam and darn in loose ends. Drape string of beads around the cozy so that it falls like a necklace, securing with stitches at a point along the seam.

This intricate pattern known as entrelac may look complicated, but the technique is surprisingly easy to master. Random yarn adds variety to this design by Ally Howard, but it is equally nice worked in a single colour.

Eggy entrelac

Materials

Colinette Cadenza 100% merino wool
(120m/131yds per 50g hank)
Approx 15g in 48 Florentina (one ball makes three cozies)
A pair of 3mm (UK11:US2–3) needles

Tension

7 sts and 9 rows to 1in (2.5cm) over st st using 3mm needles.
Use larger or smaller needles to obtain correct tension.

Special abbreviations

Kf&b: knit into front and back of stitch
Ssk: slip one stitch, then the next. Insert left needle into the front loops of the slipped stitches and knit them together from this position, through the back loops
Skpo: slip one, knit one, pass the slipped stitch over to form a left-slanting decrease
Sl1p-wise: slip one stitch purl-wise

Method

This cozy is worked from the bottom upwards, beginning with a 2-row garter stitch hem followed by the entrelac patterning. The top is shaped by decreasing just before casting off.

Cozy

Cast on 30 sts and knit 2 rows.

Base triangles

Row 1 (RS): K1, turn.
Row 2 and every alt (WS) row: Purl all sts, turn.
Row 3: Sl1, k1, turn.
Row 5: Sl1, k2, turn.
Row 7: Sl1, k3, turn.
Row 9: Sl1, k4, turn.
Row 11: Sl1, k5. Do not turn.
One base triangle is complete; beg next base triangle on next st.
Rep rows 1–11 four times to complete five base triangles.

Tier 1 – left side triangle

Row 1 (WS): P1, turn.
Row 2: Kf&b, turn.
Row 3: P1, p2tog, turn.
Row 4: K1, m1, k1, turn.
Row 5: P2, p2tog, turn.
Row 6 and all RS rows: Knit to last st, m1, k1, turn.
Row 7: P3, p2tog, turn.
Row 9: P4, p2tog, turn.

Row 11: P5, p2tog. Do not turn.
This row marks the end of the left triangle.

Tier 1 – central diamonds (right-slanting)

Row 1: Pick up and p 6 sts along edge of next triangle, slipping last picked-up st onto left needle and purling 2tog with next st, turn.
Row 2 and every alt row: K6, turn.
Row 3, 5, 7 and 9: Sl1p-wise, p4, p2tog, turn.
Row 11: Sl1p-wise, p4, p2tog. Do not turn.
This row marks the end of the first diamond. Rep rows 1–11 three times to complete central diamonds.

Tier 1 – right side triangle

Row 1 (WS): Pick up and purl 6 sts down edge of first triangle of previous row, turn.
Row 2: K6, turn.

Row 3: Sl1p-wise, p3, p2tog, turn.
Row 4: K5, turn.
Row 5: Sl1p-wise, p2, p2tog, turn.
Row 6: K4, turn.
Row 7: Sl1p-wise, p1, p2tog, turn.
Row 8: K3, turn.
Row 9: Sl1p-wise, p2tog, turn.
Row 10: K2, turn.
Row 11: P2tog, turn and transfer this st to right needle, noting that it will count as the first st of the first diamond of Tier 2.

Tier 2 – left-slanting diamonds

Row 1 (RS): Pick up and knit a further 5 sts (6 sts total) along edge of next triangle. Slip last picked-up st onto left needle, ssk, turn.
Rows 2, 4, 6, 8 and 10: P6, turn.
Rows 3, 5, 7 and 9: Sl1, k4, ssk, turn.
Row 11: Sl1, k4, ssk. Do not turn.
This row marks the end of the first diamond of Tier 2. Rep rows 1–11 to complete rem 4 diamonds, noting that the first row of each will be worked thus:
Row 1 (RS): Pick up and knit 6 sts along edge of diamond. Sl last picked-up st onto left needle, ssk, turn. Work Tier 1 again, ending with the right side triangle.

Final triangles

Row 1 (RS): Pick up and knit 6 sts along the edge of the next triangle or diamond. For the first triangle only, the st remaining counts as the first picked up stitch. Slip last picked-up st to left needle, ssk, turn.

Row 2 and all WS rows: Purl all sts, turn.

Rows 3, 5 and 7: Skpo, k to last st, ssk, turn.

Row 9: Skpo, ssk, turn.

Row 11: Sl1, ssk, then pass slipped st over so that 1 st remains.. Do not turn. The rem st will count as the first stitch of the next triangle.

Rep rows 1–11 to complete all final triangles. Fasten off last st.

Top

With 3mm needles, pick up and k 6 sts along the edge of each triangle (30 sts).

Next row: (P2tog) to end (15 sts).

Next row: Knit.

Next row: (P2tog, p1) to end (10 sts). Break off yarn leaving a long end for sewing, and thread through rem sts. Fasten off.

Making up

Join side seam using mattress stitch and matching pattern sections carefully.

What better to cover up your boiled egg with than a woolly pompom hat?
Jacqui Lewington's design is worked in rib and stocking stitch
and finished off with a jolly pompom on the top.

Mini hat

Materials

Rowan Tapestry yarn 70% wool 30% soybean protein fibre
(120m/11yds per 100g ball)
Small amount in 177 Lead Mine
3.75mm (UK9:US5) needles

Tension

Not critical

Method

The cozy is knitted from bottom to top, beginning with a 2 x 2 rib and then worked in stocking stitch. The pompom at the top is the finishing touch, made from the same yarn as the hat and stitched on.

Cozy

Cast on 36 sts.

Rows 1–8: Work in 2 x 2 rib.

Rows 9–16: Work in st st, beg with a k row.

Row 17: (K1, k2tog) to end (24 sts).

Row 18: Purl.

Rows 19–20: As rows 17–18 (16 sts).

Row 21: (K2tog) to end (8 sts).

Break off yarn leaving a tail for sewing, and thread through rem stitches. Pull tight to close top, and fasten off.

Making up

Use end of thread to sew hat side seam. Make a pompom and attach to top of hat.

Tip

This fun cozy could be worked in all sorts of different colourways to liven up your table. Bright colours with a contrasting pompom would add some morning cheer or more muted tones for a sophisticated look.

This cheerful cozy by Margaret Kelleher is perfect if you are not a morning person: its bright sunny colours should put a smile on any grumpy face.

Sunny surprise

Materials

Any DK yarns in orange and cream
A pair of 4mm (UK8:US6) needles
4mm (UK8:USG/6) hook
2 buttons for eyes
1 'lips' button for mouth
6 small golden beads
Darning needle
Sewing needle and thread

Tension

Not critical

Method

The body is knitted first from the bottom upwards using two strands of yarn together (both orange and cream) and 1 x 1 rib. The head is knitted on from there using a strand of cream yarn only and garter stitch, increasing at first and then decreasing. The seam is sewn, the head stuffed and a bow added at the neckline. Button eyes and a mouth form the face. Finally the 'rays' are added by crocheting around the head and little golden beads add sparkle.

Cozy

Body

With 4mm needles and 2 strands tog (both orange and cream), cast on 24 sts.
Rows 1–16: Work in 1 x 1 rib for body.
Rows 17–18: Work in g-st.
Break off orange yarn and cont with 1 strand of cream yarn only.

Head

Row 1: K3, (m1, k3) to end (31 sts).
Row 2 (and every foll alt row): Knit.
Row 3: K3, (m1, k4) to end (38 sts).
Row 5: K3, (m1, k5) to end (45 sts).
Rows 7–8: Knit.
Row 9: K3, (k2tog, k4) to end (38 sts).
Row 11: K3, (k2tog, k3) to end (31 sts).
Row 13: K3, (k2tog, k2) to end (24 sts).
Row 15: K3, (k2tog, k1) to end (17 sts).
Row 17: K1, (k2tog) to end (9 sts).
Row 19: K1, (k2tog) to end (5 sts).

Break off yarn leaving a tail for sewing. Thread end through rem sts to close.

Making up

Sew side seam.
Lightly stuff head with a little cream yarn, then with a length of orange yarn tie a bow around the neck to draw fabric in. Sew on buttons for eyes and mouth.

Rays

With 4mm hook and 2 strands tog (both orange and cream), join yarn to side of face.
Row 1: Mk 1 ch, work in dc all along head to other side of face.
Row 2: (Mk 10 ch, sl st into next dc) to end.
Sew a bead onto every second ray. Darn in any loose ends.

This simple design by Gina Alton is constructed from two plain rectangles. The embroidery is reminiscent of a child's drawing, depicting the most special place of all – home.

Home sweet home

Materials

Any DK yarn in navy blue, plus small amounts of DK in colours of your choice for the embroidery
A pair of 4mm (UK8:US6) needles
Darning needle

Tension

Not critical

Method

The base of this cozy is knitted in two rectangular pieces (front and back) in straightforward garter stitch with navy yarn. Contrasting colours are used to embroider onto the front piece.

Back

With 4mm needles and navy yarn cast on 20 sts.
Work 27 rows even in g-st.
Cast off loosely k-wise. Break off yarn.

Front

Work as for back but leaving a long tail for sewing up at the cast-on.

Making up

Either following the photo for guidance or embroidering your own 'drawing', use darning needle and various contrasting colours to decorate the cozy on the front piece.

When you are happy with the way it looks, use the darning needle and the long tail at cast-on to sew the front and back together. Put the two pieces together with the cast-on edge down (this will be the opening as it will stretch more easily than the cast-off edge). Sew through both layers along the other three edges and then darn in any loose ends.

The fresh colours of spring add a special charm to this simple egg cozy by Alma Suckling. It is worked in stocking stitch with a pretty flower on either side.

Spring bluebell

Materials

Any DK yarn in lilac
Any 4-ply yarns in mauve (or blue) and green
A pair each 3mm (UK11:US2–3) and 4mm (UK8:US6) needles
Two 3mm (UK11:US2-3) double-pointed needles.

Tension

Not critical

Special abbreviations

S2kpo: Slip 2, knit 1, pass slipped stitches over

Method

The cozy base is made by working two sides and joining them together with mattress stitch. Bluebells and stems are then made separately and sewn on.

Cozy

Sides (make 2 alike)

With 4mm needles and lilac, cast on 18 sts.

Rows 1–6: Work in 1 x 1 rib.

Rows 7–20: Work in st st, beg with a k row.

Row 21: K2tog, k to last 2 sts, k2tog (16 sts).

Row 22: P2tog, p to last 2 sts, p2tog (14 sts).

Row 23: As row 21 (12 sts).

Row 24: As row 22 (10 sts).

Row 25: As row 21 (8 sts).

Cast off.

Sew two sides tog with mattress stitch.

Bluebells

With 3mm needles and mauve yarn, cast on 15 sts.

Row 1 (RS): Knit.

Row 2: Purl.

Row 3: (K2tog, yo) 7 times, k1.

Rows 4–6: Beg with p row, work in st st.

Join hem

Row 7 (RS): *Insert RH needle in next st, then in back loop of corresp st of cast-on row and knit the two sts together. Rep from * to end.

Rows 8–12: Beg with a p row, work in st st.

Row 13: (S2kpo) 5 times. 5 sts.

Row 14: Purl.

Break off yarn and draw end through sts to gather them.

Stems (make 2 per flower)

With 3mm DPNs and green yarn, make a 2in (5cm) -long I-cord.

Making up

Join seam of flower setting in stem at base. Make a small tassel and attach inside flower. Darn in any loose ends.

Pollie Fenn's cozy will keep your egg warm and toasty with its blanket-like design. Autumnal colours make it perfect for those chilly mornings when you need a hearty breakfast.

Egg blanket

Materials

Any DK yarns in brown (MC), tan (CC1), beige (CC2), green (CC3) and cream (CC4)
A pair of 4mm (UK8:US6) needles
Darning needle

Tension

Not critical

Pattern notes

When changing colours, twist yarns to prevent holes appearing.

Egg blanket chart *22 sts x 24 rows*
Each square = I st and I row

Brown (MC)

Tan (CC1)

Beige (CC2)

Green (CC3)

Cream (CC4)

Note: Brown only is worked in garter stitch. Other colours are worked in stocking stitch Fair Isle.

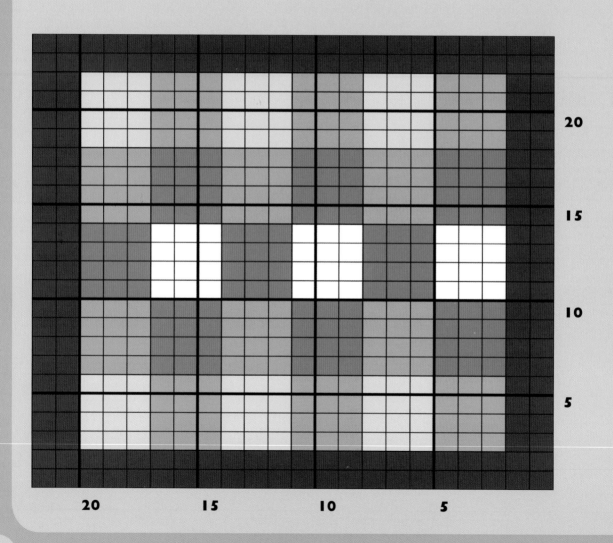

Method

The blanket cozy is knitted in two pieces, which are then sewn together. The border is made in garter stitch (all knit stitches) and the central patterned area is worked in Fair Isle.

Sides (make 2 alike)

With 4mm needles and MC cast on 22 sts.

Rows 1–2: Knit.
Row 3: K2 in MC (k3 in CC1, k3 in CC2) 3 times, k2 in MC.
Row 4: K2 in MC (p3 in CC2, p3 in CC1) 3 times, k2 in MC.
Rows 5–6: As rows 3–4.
Row 7: K2 in MC, (k3 in CC3, k3 in CC1) 3 times, k2 in MC.
Row 8: K2 in MC, (p3 in CC1, p3 in CC3) 3 times, k2 in MC.
Rows 9–10: As rows 7–8.
Row 11: K2 in MC, (k3 in CC4, k3 in CC3) 3 times, k2 in MC.
Row 12: K2 in MC, (p3 in CC3, p3 in CC4) 3 times, k2 in MC.
Rows 13–14: As rows 11–12.
Row 15: K2 in MC, (k3 in CC3, k3 in CC1) 3 times, k2 in MC.
Row 16: K2 in MC, (p3 in CC1, p3 in CC3) 3 times, k2 in MC.
Rows 17–18: As rows 15–16.
Row 19: K2 in MC, (k3 in CC1, k3 in CC2) 3 times, k2 in MC.
Row 20: K2 in MC, (p3 in CC2, p3 in CC1) 3 times, k2 in MC.

Rows 21–22: As rows 19–20.
Rows 23–24: K in MC.
Cast off k-wise.

Making up

Over-sew two pieces together on WS. Darn in ends. Turn RS out and lightly press.

Tip

In Fair Isle patterns, the yarns are carried across the back of the work. Take care not to strand yarns loosely, and do not carry over more than 3 sts. Twist together at every colour change to prevent holes.

This ingenious egg cozy designed by Jacqui Lewington
is made entirely of coiled I-cord, which is then stitched
together to form a dome shape.

Coiled cord

Materials

Oddments of any DK yarn
A pair of 3.75mm (UK9:US5) double-pointed needles
Darning needle

Tension

Not critical

Pattern notes

This method may be adapted to create many different effects. Make a single-colour I-cord cozy and then make another cord in a contrasting colour, stitching the cord down at intervals to create a 'looping' effect or even a scalloped border around the edge. Alternatively, use extra I-cord in a contrasting colour to decorate the cozy with a monogram or a flower.

Method

This cozy is made entirely from an I-cord, a long knitted tube. The shape is formed by coiling the cord around and stitching it into place.

Cozy

Make an I-cord as folls:
Cast on 4 sts.
K 1 row. Do not turn.
Slide sts to other end of needle. Pulling needle tight across back of sts, k 1 row.
Rep from * to * until I-cord is approx 50in (130cm) long, always knitting RS rows (from right to left) and changing colours as and when desired.
Break off yarn leaving a long tail for sewing, and thread end through the 4 sts to close off the tube.

Making up

Coil cord into shape, stitching together as you go.
Darn in any ends.

Tip

When changing colour, tie the two ends of yarn into a small but secure knot and tuck it into the inside of the cord as you knit, to avoid having to darn in lots of loose ends later. You could also use a variegated yarn to incorporate a variety of shades without having to change colour.

With this cheeky chick sitting on your egg it will stay warm and cozy.
Gina Alton's design is crocheted in the round for a snug fit
and incorporates cute top and tail feathers.

Spring chick

Materials

Any DK yarns in yellow, brown, orange and white
A 3.5mm (UK9:USE/4) crochet hook
Darning needle

Tension

Not critical

Method

The chick's body is worked in the round beginning with a foundation loop (floop, see page 146) and is worked from the centre top, outwards and then downwards, in spiral rounds with no joins. The eyes, beak, wings, legs and feathers for tail and head are worked separately and stitched on.

Chick

With 3.5mm hook and yellow yarn, mk floop and 1ch.

Round 1: 6dc into floop (6 sts).
Round 2: Dc2inc 6 times (12 sts).
Round 3: (1dc, dc2inc) 6 times (18 sts).
Round 4: (2dc, dc2inc) 6 times (24 sts).
Round 6: (3dc, dc2inc) 6 times (30 sts).
Rounds 7–15: Work even in dc.
Round 16: (1dc, dc2inc) to end (45 sts).
Wk 2ss to finish. Break off yarn.

Eyes (make 2 alike)

With 3.5mm hook and white yarn, mk floop and 1ch.

Round 1: 6dc into floop (6 sts).
Ss to join and then fasten off. Sew in beg end of yarn to WS of eye and trim close. With darning needle and brown yarn, stitch pupil. Break off yarn, tie beg and end tog in a double knot to secure and trim close.

Beak

With 3.5mm hook and orange yarn, mk 4ch.

Row 1: Sk1ch, 1dc, 1htr, 1tr (3 sts).
This forms an Isosceles triangle shape.
Next: Wk one round in ss around the piece, working 1ss at each corner. This will neaten the edge.
Break off yarn.

Wings (make 2 alike)

With 3.5mm hook and yellow yarn, mk 5ch.
Sk4ch and wk 6dtr into last ch st. Then mk3ch and ss into that same last ch st to finish.
Break off yarn.

Tail feathers

With 3.5mm hook and brown yarn, mk 1ch, (9ch, 1ss into very first ch st) 7 times.
Break off yarn.

Feathers for top of head

With 3.5mm hook and brown yarn, mk 1ch, (9ch, 1ss into very first ch st) 5 times.
Break off yarn.

Legs (make 2 alike)

With 3.5mm hook and brown yarn, mk 9ch.
Sk1ch, 3ss along foll 3 ch sts, (mk4ch, sk1ch, 3ss along foll 3 ch sts) twice, 5ss along rem of original chain (back to starting point).
Break off yarn.

Making up

See photos for reference when finishing off. Sew on eyes with mattress stitch. If you find the crocheted eyes too fiddly to make and sew on, try using little buttons for eyes instead. Attach wings and both sets of feathers. Lightly steam press the legs so that they lie flat and stitch to lower body. Darn in any loose ends.

Tempt your tastebuds with this delicious-looking ice cream design by Charmaine Fletcher, finished perfectly with a chocolate flake. Try using different colours so that everyone can have their favourite flavour.

Ice-cream treat

Materials

Any DK yarns in brown, cream and beige
A set of 4mm (UK8:US6) double-pointed needles
Tapestry needle
Sewing needle and thread
Tape measure
Dressmaker's pins

Tension

Not critical

Pattern notes

This cozy is designed to accommodate most egg cups but works particularly well on stemmed designs.

Ice-cream treat chart *36 sts x 14 rows*

Each square = 1 st and 1 row

Knit

Purl

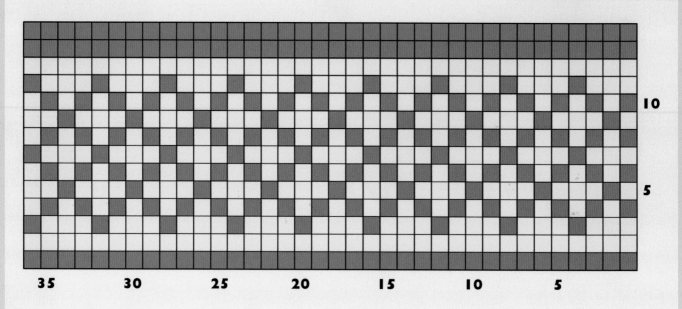

10

5

35 30 25 20 15 10 5

Method

The cone is knitted first, in the round on double-pointed needles, with a Guernsey-style pattern creating the 'waffle' texture effect. Next, the ice cream is knitted as a long I-cord tube, which is stitched into shape at finishing. Finally, the chocolate flake is knitted in a 1 x 1 rib I-cord.

Cozy

With 4mm needles and beige yarn, cast on 36 sts using the thumb method and arrange over 3 needles.

Rounds 1–14: Work in the round, following chart.
Fasten off.

Ice cream

With 4mm DPNs and cream yarn (leaving a long tail for sewing up later), cast on 5 sts using the thumb method and work an I-cord approx 27in (69cm) long. Each row is knitted right to left, with RS always facing and the yarn pulled tightly behind the work between rows, forming a knitted tube. Break off yarn. Do not cast off the 7 sts. Draw yarn through sts and pull tight into a point (this will be the whipped ice cream top).

Chocolate flake

With 4mm DPNs and brown yarn, cast on 7 sts using the thumb method and work an I-cord as above, work (k1, p1, k1, p1, k1, p1, k1) for 11 rows or until piece measures approx 1¼in (3cm). Break off yarn.

Making up

Taking the cast-on end of the cream I-cord, tuck it into the inner left-hand sided of the base and sew into place. Wind into a decreasing spiral to look like a piped ice cream, stitching into place as you go. Alternatively, tack it into place and then do the final sewing once you are happy with how it looks.

Between the second and third spiral (left-side facing) tuck in the chocolate flake and sew into place.

> ## Tip
> Coloured seed beads may be sewn on to resemble candy sprinkles instead of the chocolate flake.

This delicate design by Lesley Fidler is crocheted in mohair for a soft, fluffy effect. It's so pretty, it will match your vintage china perfectly.

Bell flower

Materials

Oddments of DK mohair in cream, light pink and green
4mm (UK8:USG/6) hook

Tension

16 sts and 12 rows to 4in (10cm) over tr st using 4mm hook.
Use larger or smaller needles to obtain correct tension.

Pattern notes

When counting stitches, the 3ch that starts the round is *not* counted as a stitch.

Method

This fluffy cozy is crocheted in the round, using a single strand of yarn throughout. The lining is worked first from the top down and then the outside is worked, also from the top down and starting with a curly wurly. The outside is then slipped over the lining, and the petal edging added to hold the two pieces together.

Cozy lining

With cream, mk a sl-knot and 3ch.

Round 1: Work 15tr into the sl-knot, finishing with a ss to the top of the ch-3 at the beg of round to join (15 tr). Draw the sl-knot tight and darn in the yarn end to secure it.

Round 2: Mk3ch, (2tr, tr2inc) 5 times, join round with a ss (20 tr).

Round 3: Mk3ch, (4tr, tr2inc) 4 times, join round with a ss (24 tr).

Round 4: Mk3ch, (5tr, tr2inc) 4 times, join round with a ss (28 tr).

Rounds 5–7: Mk3ch, work 1tr into each st to end, join round with a ss. Break off yarn.

Outer cozy

Curly wurly

With green, mk8ch.

Work 5tr into 4th ch from hook, 5tr into each of the next 3 ch sts, then 15tr into the final ch st.

Join the 15 tr into a round with a ss into the top of the first of the 15 (this counts as round 1).

There should be a curly wurly sticking out of the top of the round.

Main piece

Change to pink yarn.

Round 2: Mk3ch, (2tr, tr2inc) 5 times, join round with a ss (20 tr).

Round 3: Mk3ch, (4tr, tr2inc) 4 times, join round with a ss (24 tr).

Round 4: Mk3ch, (5tr, tr2inc) 4 times, join round with a ss (28 tr).

Rounds 5–6: Mk3ch, work 1tr into each st to end, join round with a ss. Change to cream yarn.

Round 7: Mk3ch, work 1tr into each st to end, join round with a ss.

Petal edging

Slip the lining inside the main piece. With cream yarn and working each st into the edge of both the lining and the main piece to join, work as folls:

Mk1ch, (sk1st, 6dtr into next st, sk1st, 1dc into foll st) 7 times, working the final dc into the base of the 1ch. Break off yarn.

Making up

Darn in ends.

Susan Hunt's delightful octopus egg cozy will be
a hit with all sealife-lovers. The dangling legs are knitted
in a strip and attached to the body later.

Olly octopus

Materials

Any DK yarn in variegated blue mix
A pair of 3.25mm (UK10:US3) needles
Darning needle
Small piece of white felt for eyes
Black embroidery thread for pupils of eyes
White thread to sew the felt eyes to the octopus
Sewing needle

Tension

Not critical

Special abbreviations

MB: make bobble
(K1, p1, k1, p1) all in next st, turn, p4, turn, k4, turn, p4, (sl2, k2,
pass 2 slipped sts over)

Method

The octopus body is made first, knitted in rows from the bottom up. First in moss stitch (plus two bobbles for eye backings) and then changing to garter stitch when decreasing for the top. The legs are made in a garter stitch strip, which is then sewn onto the base of the body. The eyes are made from white felt and black embroidery thread, and attached to the bobbles.

Body

With 3.25mm needles and blue yarn, cast on 34 sts.

Rows 1–5: Work in moss stitch. On the next row two 'bobbles' for the eye backings. will be made

Row 6: M-st 13, MB, m-st 6, MB, m-st to end.

Rows 7–18: Work even in m-st. Shape top (working now in g-st)

Row 19: K1, (k2tog) to last st, k1 (18 sts).

Row 20: K1, (k2tog) to last st, k1 (10 sts).

Row 21: K1, (k2tog) to last st, k1 (6 sts).

Break off yarn and thread end through rem sts to close.

Legs

With 3.25mm needles and blue yarn, cast on 3 sts.

Row 1: Knit.

Row 2: K3, cast on 1 st (4 sts).

Row 3: Knit across all 4 sts.

Row 4: K4, cast on 10 sts (14 sts).

Rows 5–6: Knit across all 14 sts.

Row 7: Cast off 10 sts, k to end (4 sts).

Row 8: Knit across all 4 sts.

Row 9: Cast off 1 st, k to end (3 sts).

Row 10: Knit.

One leg complete.

Rep these 10 rows 7 times, to complete all 8 legs. Cast off.

Making up

With darning needle, sew back seam of body. Sew the leg strip around the base of the body. Cut out small white felt circles for eye and satin stitch black pupils onto them. Place the felt eyes on the eye backings (the bobbles) and carefully stitch into place with sewing needle and thread.

Start the day with a boiled egg and a reminder to eat more fruit!
This juicy red apple by Gina Alton is a bright and fun addition
to the breakfast table.

An apple a day

Materials

Any DK yarns in red, green and brown
A 3.5mm (UK9:USE/4) crochet hook
Darning needle

Tension

Not critical

Method

The apple is worked in the round beginning with a foundation loop (floop, see page 146) and is worked from the centre top, outwards and then downwards, in spiral rounds with no joins. The 'dimple' at the top, where the leaf and stem are joined, is created by turning the cozy inside out and then making a few stitches through the fabric to pucker it. Finally, the leaf shape is created by working both sides of a short chain with varying-sized stitches. The stem is simply a chain with one row of slip stitches.

Apple

With 3.5mm hook and red yarn, mk floop and 1ch.

Round 1: 6dc into floop (6 sts).
Round 2: Dc2inc 6 times (12 sts).
Round 3: Wk even in dc.
Round 4: (1dc, dc2inc) 6 times (18 sts).
Round 5: (2dc, dc2inc) 6 times (24 sts).
Round 6: (3dc, dc2inc) 6 times (30 sts).
Round 7: (4dc, dc2inc) 6 times (36 sts).
Round 8: (5dc, dc2inc) 6 times (42 sts).
Rounds 9–19: Work even in dc.
Round 20: (5dc, dc2tog) 6 times (36 sts).
Wk 2ss to finish. Break off yarn.

Leaf

With 3.5mm hook and green yarn, mk 6ch.
Row 1: Sk1ch, 1ss, 1dc, 1htr, 1tr. There is one ch st left: mk 2ch and ss into that last ch st. The first half of the leaf is complete.
Now rotate leaf clockwise, to work along the underside of the chain for the second half of the leaf.
Row 2: Mk 2ch and sk first ch st, then 1tr, 1htr, 1dc, 1ss along the rest of the ch. Next you are going to work the final row, which is simply slip stitch along the original chain between rows 1 and 2.
Row 3: Mk 1ch, rotate leaf again to change direction and work 1ss into each ch st to end.
Break off yarn.

Stem

With 3.5mm hook and brown yarn, mk 6ch.
Row 1: Sk1ch, 5ss.
Break off yarn.

Making up

Turn apple inside out. With darning needle and red yarn, make a few stitches back and forth through the fabric at round 3 (this creates a pucker effect at the top where the stem and leaf will be joined). Darn in any loose ends on the apple and turn RS outwards again. Sew on leaf and stem, and darn in ends.

Humpty Dumpty sat on the wall, Humpty Dumpty had a great fall...
Alexandra McKee's design is based on the classic childhood rhyme
that everyone knows and loves.

Humpty Dumpty

Materials

Any 4-ply cotton yarns in blue, beige, orange and green
A set of four 3mm (UK11:US2–3) double-pointed needles
Tapestry needle

Tension

28 sts and 38 rows to 4in (10cm) over patt using
3mm needles. Use larger or smaller needles to obtain
correct tension

Method

Humpty's body is made first, beginning with blue in a 2 x 2 rib and then st st in beige with decreases at the top to close. The I-cord legs are then made separately and sewn to the body, then the feet are made from rectangular st st pieces and attached to the legs.

Cozy

With blue yarn cast on 42 sts and divide between 3 DPNs. 14 sts each. Place marker at beg of round and work in 2 x 2 rib for 7 rounds.

Round 8: (K5, k2tog) to last st, k1 (36 sts).

Round 9: (K4, k2tog) to last st, k1 (30 sts).

Round 10: (K3, k2tog) to last st, k1 (24 sts).

Round 11: (K2, k2tog) to last st, k1 (18 sts).

Round 12: (K1, k2tog) to last st, k1 (12 sts).

Round 13: (K2tog) to end (6 sts).

Round 14: (K2tog) to end (3 sts).

Thread yarn through 3 rem sts to tie off.

Legs (make 2 alike)

With orange cast on 6 sts and knit an I-cord 1½in (3.5cm) long, or desired length.

Insert yarn through the 6 sts to tie off and secure.

Stitch legs to bottom of egg cozy, leaving about ½in (1cm) space between legs.

Feet (make 2 alike)

With green cast on 8 sts. Work in st st stitch for 10 rows.

Cast off.

With WS facing (purl side), fold rectangle in half, long side vertical. Sew together short ends and two-thirds along the length of long end, leaving a hole. Turn inside out. Stick leg into foot and sew around to secure.

Making up

Using yarn leftovers from green and orange, embroider eyes and a mouth on Humpty's head. Darn in any loose ends.

Wake up to a posy of violets on your breakfast table every morning with this pretty design by Ally Howard. The garter stitch fabric is thick enough to keep your egg snug, and the picot edge adds a touch of delicacy.

Devon violets

Materials

Any DK yarns in light green, dark green, violet and yellow
A pair of 4mm (UK8:US6) needles
3mm (UK11:USC2–D/3) hook
Darning needle

Tension

Not critical

Method

The cozy itself is knitted in rows from the bottom up, beginning with a picot hem and then continuing in garter stitch. The flowers are crocheted in the round and the leaves knitted in garter stitch rows. The seam of the cozy is sewn and then the flowers and leaves stitched on for decoration.

Cozy

With 4mm needles and light green, cast on 37 sts.

Rows 1–2: Beg with a k row, work in st st.

Row 3 (picot edge): K1, (yf, k2tog) to end.

Rows 4–6: Work in st st.

Row 7 (joining hem): (Knit tog next st and 1 st from cast-on edge) to end.

Row 8: Work in st st.

Change to g-st and work until piece measures 3½in (9cm) or length required.

Shape top

Row 1: K5, (k2tog, k4) to last 2 sts, k2tog (31 sts).

Row 2: Knit.

Row 3: K4, (k2tog, k3) to last 2 sts, k2tog (25 sts).

Row 4: Knit.

Row 5: K3, (k2tog, k2) to last 2 sts, k2tog (19 sts).

Next row: Knit.

Next row: K2, (k2tog, k1) to last 2 sts, k2tog (13 sts).

Next row: Knit.

Next row: K1, (k2tog) to end (7 sts).

Next row: Knit.

Break off yarn leaving a long end and thread through rem sts to fasten off.

Violets (make 6)

With 3mm hook and yellow, make a loop of yarn and work 10dc into loop. Join dc with a ss to form a ring. Pull loop tightly closed.

Change to violet yarn.

Next round: *Work (1dc, 1htr, 1tr, 1htr, 1dc) into first dc, ss into second dc. Rep from * to end, then ss to first dc to join the round.

Fasten off, leaving a tail for sewing.

Leaves (make 4 or 5)

With 4mm needles and dark green, cast on 2 sts.

Row 1: Inc in first st, k1 (3 sts).

Row 2: Inc in first st, k2 (4 sts).

Row 3: Inc in first st, k3 (5 sts).

Row 4: Inc in first st, k4 (6 sts).

Row 5: Inc in first st, k5 (7 sts).

Row 6: Inc in first st, k6 (8 sts).

Row 7: (K1, sl1, psso), k to last 2 sts, k2tog (6 sts).

Cast off.

Break off yarn leaving a tail for sewing.

Making up

With darning needle join side seam of cozy, matching garter stitch ridges carefully. Attach leaves and violets to top of cozy – not too tidily – to resemble a bunch of freshly picked violets. Darn in any loose ends.

Simple crochet is used for this design by Anita Ursula Nycs, which makes it super-fast to work – and no sewing up is necessary!

Creative crochet

Materials

Any DK yarns in green, beige, light pink and hot pink
3.5mm (UK9:USE/4) and 4mm (UK8:USG/6) hooks
Darning needle
Lining material, sewing needle and thread (optional)

Tension

Not critical

Special abbreviations

Dc2inc: 2 double crochet into next stitch (to increase)

Method

The base is made first by crocheting two sides and joining them with slip stitch. A border is worked around the seam, then embellishment and embroidery added for decoration. A top loop completes the piece.

Cozy

Base (make 2 pieces)

With 4mm hook and green yarn, mk 11 ch.

Row 1: Sk 1 ch, dc to end. 10 dc.

Row 2: Ch 1 (t-ch), dc to end.

Rep row 2 until piece measures 2in (5cm).

Fasten off.

Make a second piece, then join the two together with sl st.

Seam border

With 3.5mm hook, join light pink yarn and mk 1 ch.

Row 1: Work 1 dc into each sl st around seam.

Row 2: Work dc2inc into each dc.

Fasten off.

Lower border

With 3.5mm hook and beige yarn, work 2 rounds in sl st around base. Change to light pink yarn and work 2 further rounds in dc.

Fasten off.

Making up

Embroider the central flower by working ch sts through the fabric in a petal pattern.

With sewing needle and thread, attach lining material (if desired).

Top loop

With 3.5mm hook and light pink, join yarn to top of cozy, mk 4 ch, sl st to cozy to form loop and fasten off.

Darn in any loose ends.

Boiled eggs are not just for breakfast: they are also perfect for a proper high tea. Imogen Cox has chosen sugar-pink yarn and a fluffy rose for this delicate design that will complement your prettiest china.

Party cake

Materials

Any cotton or cotton-mix DK yarn in pale pink (approx 20g)
Oddments of mohair or fluffy 3- or 4-ply yarn in magenta
Oddments of DK wool yarn in variegated green
A pair each 3mm (UK11:US2–3) and 4mm (UK8:US6)
needles

Tension

6 sts and 8 rows to 1in (2.5cm) over st st using 4mm needles.
Use larger or smaller needles to obtain correct tension.

Method

The shell-patterned cozy is knitted first from the bottom up, decreasing at the top to close. The flower is knitted as a flat piece, which is later curled to form a rose shape and then stitched into place. The two leaves are knitted as a single-shaped piece in garter stitch and joined with a narrow band of knitting. The flower is sewn onto this band and then it and the leaves are stitched onto the top of the cozy.

Cozy

With pale pink DK and cable cast-on, cast on 39 sts and work in patt as folls:

Shell pattern

Row 1 (RS): K2, (yf, k8, yf, k1) to last st, k1.

Row 2: K3, (p8, k3) to end.

Row 3: K3, (yf, k8, yf, k3) to end.

Row 4: K4, (p8, k5) to last 4 sts, k4.

Row 5: K4, (yf, k8, yf, k5) to last 4 sts, k4.

Row 6: K5, (p8, k7) to last 5 sts, k5.

Row 7: K5, *slip next 4 sts k-wise then pass the third, second and first of these sts, one at a time, over the fourth stitch slipped and then k this st; return to sts on left needle and slip the second, third and fourth st, one at a time, over the first st and then k this st; k7. Rep from * to end, ending last rep k5 (39 sts).

Row 8: Knit.

These 8 rows form the pattern.

Rep rows 1–8 three times.

Shape top

Next row: (K2tog) to last 3 sts, k3 tog (19 sts).

Next row: (P2tog) to last 3 sts, p3tog (9 sts).

Break off yarn leaving a long end for sewing up and thread through rem sts to close top.

Flower

Using 3mm needles and magenta yarn, cast on 30 sts.

Row 1: Knit.

Row 2: K10 sts, turn.

Row 3: P10 sts.

Row 4: K20 sts, turn.

Row 5: P20 sts.

Row 6: Knit all sts.

Row 7: Purl all sts.

Cast off.

Leaves

Using 3mm needles and oddment of variegated green yarn, cast on 2 sts and work in g-st throughout.

Row 1: Knit.

Row 2 (inc): *Inc in first st, k to end.

Rep row 2 until there are 6 sts on needle.

Knit 2 rows.

Next row (dec): Skpo, k to end.

Rep dec row until there are 2 sts on needle.*

Knit 4 rows on these 2 sts.

Now rep from * to * to produce the second leaf, which will be joined to the first by a narrow strip of knitting.

Next row: K2tog.

Fasten off.

Making up

Join side seam of cozy using mattress stitch and matching pattern carefully. To form the flower shape, beg at narrow end of magenta knitted piece and with RS of st st to the outside, roll up the flower section to form a rose shape, catching stitches in place as you go. Attach 'strap' of leaf to back of rose. Arrange rose and leaf on top of cozy and catch stitch in place.

> ### Tip
> *The row that forms the top of the shell is a little tricky, but you will soon get the hang of it!*

This cuddlesome character by Anita Ursula Nycs is just the thing to complete your breakfast table – you could say he's a 'bear' necessity.

Bear hug

Materials

Any Aran yarn in beige
Any DK yarns in black for ears and mouth, and pink
for the bow
3.5mm (UK9:USE/4) and 4mm (UK8:USG/6) hooks
Darning needle
Lining material, sewing needle and thread (optional)

Tension

Not critical

Special abbreviations

Dc2(3)tog: Double crochet 2(3) together (to decrease)

Method

The body is made first by crocheting two sides and joining them with slip stitch. The ears are made from two pieces each which are stitched together and sewn on. The features are embroidered, and then the bow crocheted and sewn on.

Cozy

Body (make 2 pieces)

With 4mm hook and beige yarn, mk 11 ch.

Row 1: Sk 1 ch, dc to end. 10 dc.

Row 2: Ch 1 (t-ch), dc to end.

Rep row 2 until piece measures 2in (5cm).

Fasten off.

Make a second piece, then join the two together with sl st.

Ears (make 4 pieces in total)

With 3.5mm hook, mk 5 ch.

Row 1: Sk 1 ch, dc to end (4 dc).

Row 2: Ch 1 (t-ch), dc to end.

Rep row 2 until piece measures 1in (2.5cm).

Next row: (Dc2tog) twice (2 sts).

Fasten off.

When all four ear pieces are complete, sew two together for one ear and the other two together for the second ear. Sew ears onto body.

Eyes

With black yarn, embroider features.

Bow (make 2 pieces)

With 3.5mm hook and pink yarn, mk 4 ch.

Row 1: Sk 1 ch, dc to end (3 dc).

Rows 2–4: Ch 1 (t-ch), dc to end.

Row 5: Dc3tog.

Fasten off.

When both pieces are made, sew the points (at row 5) tog, then work 1 round of dc around the edge. Wrap some pink yarn around the middle of the bow and sew onto cozy body.

Making up

With 4mm hook and beige yarn, work 2 rows of dc around base of cozy. With sewing needle and thread, attach lining material (if desired).

Columns of twisted stitches add something special
to this classic cozy designed by Gina Alton. The rich blue
denim will look great on any table setting.

Denim twist

Materials

Rowan Denim DK 100% pure indigo dyed cotton
(93m/100yds before washing per 50g ball)
1 x 50g ball in 229 Memphis
A pair of 4mm (UK8:US6) needles
Cable needle
Darning needle

Tension

Not critical

Special abbreviations

T3R: Twist 3 right (slip next 2 sts onto cable needle and hold
to back of work, k next st, then k the 2 sts from cable needle).

Method

This denim cozy features a garter stitch border at the cast-on edge, columns of twisted stitches separated by reverse stocking stitch and a gathered ruffled top at the cast-off edge.

Cozy

With 4mm needles cast on 38 sts.

Border

Work 4 rows even in g-st.

Beg twist patt

Row 1 (RS) (twist row): K1, (T3R, p3) to last st, k1.

Row 2: K1, (k3, p3) to last st, k1.

Rows 3–16: Rep rows 1–2 seven times. 8 twist rows in all.

Row 17 (RS): K1, (T3R, p3tog) to last st, k1 (26 sts).

Row 18: K1, (k1, p3) to last st, k1.

Cast off k-wise.

Fasten off, leaving an 8in (20cm) tail for sewing.

Making up

With darning needle and WS facing, draw needle through each k st of last WS row (row 18). Pull tight to close into a ruffled top, and secure with a double knot. Sew side seam and darn in ends. Machine-wash the cozy before use – it will shrink in length a bit in the first wash.

Tip

Denim shrinks somewhat length-wise in the first wash. Machine-wash the cozy before use, to shrink it to its finished size and to remove excess dye.

Have one of the Queen's Guards to watch over your boiled egg!
Tracey Douthwaite's smart soldier design comes complete with
the iconic bearskin hat.

Eggy soldier

Materials

Any DK yarns in red, black and white and yellow

A pair of 4mm (UK8:US6) needles

A 4mm (UK8:USG/6) hook

Small amount of thread in red and blue

Darning needle

Sewing needle

Tension

Not critical

Method

The soldier's body is the base of this cozy, knitted from the bottom upwards in red stocking stitch with a black band of reverse stocking stitch in the middle. Decreases are worked for the shoulders, changed to white for the face and increased again for the head. For 4 rows two colours are used for the helmet and face simultaneously, then black only finishes the tall hat. Arms and legs are worked in crochet with red and black respectively, and sewn on.

Body

With 4mm needles and red yarn cast on 24 sts.
Rows 1–7: Beg with a k row, work in st st.

Change to black yarn.
Row 8: Work in st st.
Rows 9–11: Work in rev st st.
Row 12: Work in st st.
Change to red yarn.
Rows 13–18: Work in st st.
Row 19: (K2tog) to end (12 sts).
Change to white yarn, leaving a long tail for drawing together the neck later.
Row 20 (WS): Purl.
Row 21: K1, m1, k to last st, m1, k1 (14 sts).
Row 22: Purl.
Join in black.
Row 23: K5 in black, k4 in white, k5 in black (twisting yarns at the colour change points to avoid leaving a hole).
Row 24: P5 in black, p4 in white, p5 in black.
Row 25–26: As rows 23–24.
Row 27: As row 23.
Break off white yarn.
Rows 28–35: With black only, work in st st.
Row 36: (P2tog) 7 times (7 sts).
Row 37: (K2tog) 3 times, k1 (4 sts).
Break off black yarn and pull thread through rem stitches to close top.
Sew back seam along hat and body, stuffing hat with a little yarn as you go. Wrap beg end of white thread around neck, pull tightly and knot to secure. Sew on eyes with blue thread, mouth with red thread and helmet strap with black yarn.

Legs (make 2 alike)

With 4mm hook and black yarn, mk10ch.
Row 1: Sk1ch, 9dc.
Break off yarn and sew leg to body.

Arms (make 2 alike)

With 4mm hook and red yarn, mk10ch.
Row 1: Sk1ch, 9dc.
Break off yarn and sew arm to body.

Making up

Darn in any loose ends.
Sew 4 'buttons' on with darning needle and yellow yarn.

Garter-stitch stripes in rainbow-coloured random yarn add interest to this simple, quickly-worked design by Elaine Thomas. To make a jolly coordinated set for each member of the family, use a different bright background colour for each cozy.

Sunshine and rainbows

Materials

Paton's Fairytale Colour 4 Me DK 100% pure new wool
(90m/98yds per 50g ball)
Approx 10g in 4960 yellow (A)
Sirdar Bonus Flash DK (280m/306yds per 100g ball)
Approx 10g in 909 Jamboree (B)
A pair of 4mm (UK8:US6) needles

Tension

6 sts and 8 rows to 1in (2.5cm) over st st using 4mm needles.
Use larger or smaller needles to obtain correct tension.

Method

This cozy is knitted in rows from the bottom hem upwards, in alternating bands of stocking stitch and garter stitch. Stitches are decreased to draw in the top, then in a final band stitches are increased again for the 'doughnut' detail at the top which rolls over as reverse stocking stitch.

Cozy

With A, cast on 33 sts and work
3 rows in g-st.
*Work 2 rows in st st.
Join in B and work 4 rows g-st.
Rep from * twice more.

Shape top

Row 1: K1, (k1, k2tog) to last 2 sts, k2
(23 sts).
Row 2: Purl.
Row 3: K1, (k1, k2tog) to last st, k1
(16 sts).
Row 4: Purl.
Row 5: (K1, k2tog) to last st, k1 (11 sts).
Row 6: Purl.
Join in B.
Next row: Inc in every st to end
(22 sts).
Beg with a p row, work 6 rows st st on
these 22 sts. Cast off.

Making up

Join side seam using mattress stitch and matching pattern sections carefully. Run a double length of yarn round the top of the cozy, just below the reversed stocking stitch top section, to draw the stitches into a smaller circle. Allow the last rows of reversed stocking stitch to roll over in a 'doughnut' shape.

Kids will love this quirky character, who will ensure your boiled eggs never get icy cold. Sheila Woolrich's design is worked in garter stitch and topped off with a jaunty bell.

Peggy penguin

Materials

Any DK yarns in black, white, orange, yellow and blue
A pair each 3.25mm (UK10:US3) and 4mm (UK8:US6) needles
2 'wobble-eye' buttons
1 small bell for the hat

Tension

Not critical

Method

The penguin's body is knitted in rows first, from bottom to top, with the colour changing to blue for the hat. The body and hat seams are sewn and the bell attached to the tip of the hat. The tummy is knitted next and sewn on; followed by the beak, eyes, wings and feet.

Body

With 4mm needles and black yarn, cast on 30 sts and work 22 rows in g-st.

Dec for top

Row 1: (K4, k2tog) to last 6 sts, k6 (26 sts).

Row 2 (and foll even rows): Knit.

Row 3: K3, (k2tog, k4) 3 times, k2tog, k3 (22 sts).

Break off black yarn leaving a tail for sewing.

Now change to blue yarn for hat.

Row 5: K4, (k2tog, k2) 3 times, k2tog, k4 (18 sts).

Row 7: K2, (k2tog, k2) to end (14 sts).

Row 9: K3, (k2tog) 4 times, k3 (10 sts).

Row 11: (K2tog) to end (5 sts).

Rows 12–13: Knit.

Row 14: K2tog, k1, k2tog (3 sts).

Break off yarn leaving a tail for sewing and thread end through rem sts to close.

Join back seam of body in black.

Sew seam of hat in blue and attach bell to top.

Tummy

With 4mm needles and white yarn, cast on 9 sts.

Row 1: Knit.

Row 2: Inc 1 st, k to end (10 sts).

Rows 3–10: Knit.

Row 11: K to last 2 sts, k2tog (9 sts).

Row 12: Knit.

Cast off loosely.

Fasten off, leaving a tail for sewing.

Sew tummy onto centre front of body.

Beak

With 3.25mm needles and orange yarn, cast on 6 sts.

Row 1: Knit.

Row 2: Purl.

Row 3: K2tog, k2, k2tog (4 sts).

Row 4: Purl.

Row 5: (K2tog) twice (2 sts).

Row 6: K2tog.

Break off yarn leaving a tail for sewing. Stuff slightly with a little spare orange yarn and sew into place above tummy.

Eyes

With 3.25mm needles and white yarn, cast on 12 sts. Break off yarn and thread end through these 12 sts, pulling tight to form a circle. Sew on button eye onto this backing then attach to penguin. Repeat for second eye.

Note: If you do not have any button eyes, just embroider the pupils in black yarn.

Wings

With 4mm needles and black yarn, cast on 8 sts.

Rows 1–8: Work in g-st.

Row 9: K2tog, k4, k2tog (6 sts).

Row 10: Knit

Row 11: K2tog, k2, k2tog (4 sts).

Rows 12–13: Knit.

Cast off.

Break off yarn, leaving a tail for sewing.

Thread yarn through cast-on edge and gather it slightly.

Attach wings to penguin body, level with the top of the eye and about ⅜in (1cm) away.

Feet

With 4mm needles and yellow yarn, cast on 5 sts.

Rows 1–2: Knit.

Break off yarn leaving a tail for sewing.

Thread end through sts and pull together.

Sew to penguin body.

Making up

Darn in any loose ends.

A naked egg!

Techniques

How to make your boiled egg decent

Getting started

Size

The instructions given are to fit a standard size egg. If you would like to make a larger egg cozy, try changing the needles for a bigger size and work a few more rows to make the sides longer. If you'd like to make a smaller cozy, a change to smaller needles may bring down the dimensions sufficiently.

Tension

Variations in tension can have a noticeable effect on the size of the finished cozy. If you are a new knitter, it is a good idea to start a habit that will save a lot of time in the end: work a swatch using the chosen yarn and needles. These can be labelled and filed for future reference. The tension required is given at the beginning of each pattern or stated if tension is not critical for that particular pattern.

Materials and equipment

Needles and hooks

Most of the designs in this book are worked back and forth on standard knitting needles. Bamboo needles are useful if you are using a rough-textured yarn as they are very smooth and will help to prevent snags. You may also need double-pointed or circular needles. Where crochet hooks are used, these are standard metal hooks that are widely available.

Yarn

Cozies may be made in a huge variety of yarns. Wool or wool-mix yarns have the best insulating properties, but cotton or silk are also good. If you are using acrylic yarn, you may prefer to choose one of the thicker designs, or one that has a lining. Cozies are also an ideal way to use up oddments of yarn.

Substituting yarn

It is relatively simple to substitute different yarns for any of the projects in this book. One way to do this is to work out how many wraps per inch (wpi) the yarn produces (see table). It is important to check tension, so begin by working a tension swatch. Then wind the yarn closely, in a single layer, round a rule or similar object, and count how many 'wraps' it produces to an inch (2.5cm). For a successful result, choose a yarn that produces twice, or slightly more than twice, the number of wraps per inch as there are stitches per inch in the tension swatch.

Tension required	Number of wraps per inch produced by yarn
8 sts per in (4-ply/fingering)	16–18 wraps per inch
6.5 sts per in (DK/sport)	13–14 wraps per inch
5.5 sts per in (Chunky/worsted)	11–12 wraps per inch

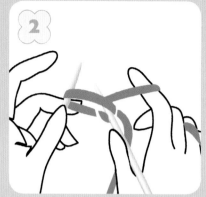

Knitting techniques

Simple cast-on

1 Form a slip knot on the left needle. Insert the right needle into the loop and wrap yarn round it as shown.

2 Pull the yarn through the first loop to create a new one.

3 Slide it on to the left-hand needle. There are now 2 sts on the left needle. Continue in this way until you have the required number of sts.

Cable cast-on

For a firmer edge, cast on the first 2 sts as shown above. When casting on the third and subsequent sts, insert the needle *between* the cast-on sts on the left needle, wrap the yarn round and pull through to create a loop. Slide the loop on to the left needle. Repeat to end.

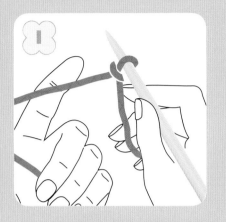 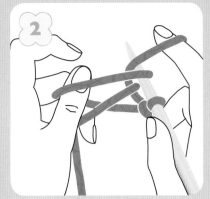 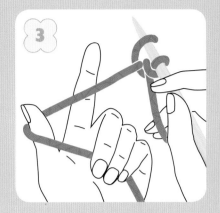

Thumb method cast-on

1 Make a slip knot some way from the end of the yarn and place on the needle. Pull the knot tight.

2 Hold needle in right hand and wrap the loose tail end round the left thumb, from front to back. Push the needle point through the thumb loop from front to back. Wind ball end of yarn round needle from left to right.

3 Pull the loop through thumb loop, then remove thumb. Gently pull the new loop tight using the tail yarn. Rep until the desired number of sts are on the needle.

Casting off

1 Knit 2 sts on to the right-hand needle, then slip the first st over the second st and let it drop off the needle so that 1 st remains.

2 Knit another st so you have 2 sts on the right-hand needle again.

Rep process until there is only 1 st on the left needle. Break yarn and thread through rem st to fasten off.

Knit stitch

1 Hold the needle with the cast-on sts in your left hand. Place the tip of the empty right needle into the first st and wrap the yarn round as for casting on.

2 Pull the yarn through to create a new loop.

3 Slip the newly-made st on to the right needle.

Continue in the same way for each st on the left-hand needle.

To start a new row, turn the work to swap the needles and repeat steps.

Purl stitch

1 Hold the yarn at the front of the work as shown.

2 Place the right needle into the first st from front to back. Wrap the yarn round the needle in an anti-clockwise direction as shown.

3 Bring the needle back through the st and pull through.

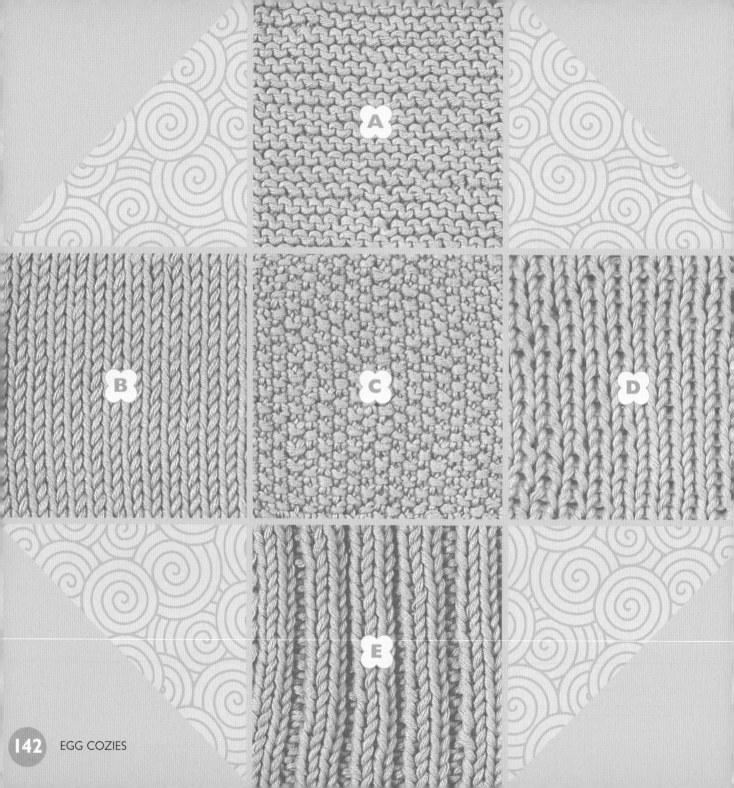

A Garter stitch (g-st)

Knit every row.

B Stocking stitch (st st)

Knit on RS rows and purl on WS rows.
Reverse stocking stitch (rev st st): Purl on RS rows and knit on WS rows.

C Moss stitch (m-st)

With an even number of sts:
Row 1: (k1, p1) to end.
Row 2: (p1, k1) to end.
Rep rows 1 and 2 for pattern.

With an odd number of sts:
Row 1: *k1, p1, rep from * to last st, k1.
Rep to form pattern.

D Single (1 x 1) rib

With an even number of sts:
Row 1: *K1, p1* rep to end.
Rep for each row.

With an odd number of sts:
Row 1: *K1, p1, rep from * to last st, k1.
Row 2: *P1, k1, rep from * to last st, p1.

E Double (2 x 2) rib

With a multiple of 4 sts:
Row 1: *K2, p2, rep from * to end.
Rep for each row.

Working with double-pointed needles (dpns)

Using double-pointed needles is a way of working in the round and usually involves using four or five needles. One needle is always kept aside as the 'working needle'.

easier to do this on one needle and then slip them across afterwards. Put a stitch marker on the first stitch so that you can see where the round starts and ends.

1 Divide the number of stitches to be cast on by the number of needles (not including the working needle). So if using a set of four dpns, divide the number of stitches by three. If you only have a small number of stitches to cast on then it may be

2 Knit across the stitches from each needle, taking care not to twist the cast-on row and slipping the stitch marker across when it is reached. As you empty each needle it becomes your working needle for the next section. Continue working the stitches in this way as required.

Intarsia

Blocks of colour are created by using the intarsia technique of twisting the yarns together at the back of the work with each colour change (see diagram). It is better to use bobbins than whole balls to prevent tangling. They are smaller and can hang at the back of the work out of the way. Once finished, ends are woven in at the back, and pressing under a damp cloth will help to neaten any distorted stitches.

Reading charts

Most charts are shown in squares, with each square representing one stitch. Charts are usually marked in sections of ten stitches, which makes counting easier.

When working in stocking stitch on straight needles, read the chart from right to left on knit (RS) rows and from left to right on purl (WS) rows. Check carefully after every purl row to make sure that the pattern stitches are in the correct position.

Crochet techniques

Foundation loop (floop)

Some egg cozies are worked in continuous spiral rounds with no joining slip stitches or turning chains. These spiral rounds are begun with a foundation loop (floop).

Yarn over hook twice, pull through to form loop, do not tighten as you will be working your first round into this floop.

Round 1: Make 1 chain stitch (mk1ch), then work 6 double crochet stitches (6dc) into the floop. Pull beginning end of yarn to tighten the floop. Continue straight onto the next round, without making a join or turning chain.

Round 2: Work a dc2inc into each stitch of round 1.

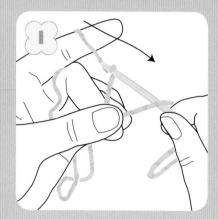

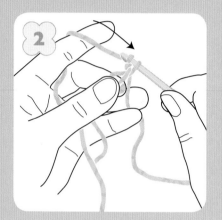

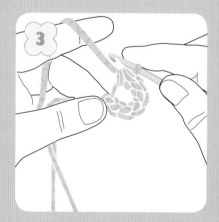

Chain stitch (ch)

1 With hook in right hand and yarn resting over middle finger of left hand, pull yarn taut. Take hook under, then over yarn.

2 Pull the hook and yarn through the loop while holding slip knot steady. Rep to form a foundation row of chain stitch (ch).

Double crochet (dc)

1 Place hook into a st. Wrap yarn round hook and draw the loop back through the work towards you.

2 There should now be two loops on the hook. Wrap yarn round hook again, then draw through both loops, leaving one loop on the hook one double crochet (dc) now complete. Rep to continue row.

Half-treble (h-tr)

Wrap yarn round hook, then place into a stitch. Wrap yarn round hook, then draw the loop through (3 loops now on hook). Wrap yarn round hook again and draw through the 3 loops (one loop remains on hook).

Treble (tr)

Follow instructions for half treble until there are 3 loops on the hook. Catch yarn with hook and draw through 2 of the loops, then catch yarn again and draw through rem 2 loops.

Double treble

Work as for a treble, but wrap yarn round hook twice before placing in st (four loops on hook). Work off loops two at a time.

Triple treble

Work as for a treble, but wrap yarn round hook three times before placing in st (five loops on hook). Work off loops two at a time.

Note: these are very tall stitches.

Stitch tips

Chain stitch (**A**) is the usual base
for other crochet stitches and is also useful
for making simple ties. Double crochet (**B**)
produces a dense fabric that is ideal for
lining, and single rows are ideal for edging.
Crochet worked in half-treble (**C**) and
treble (**D**) stitch has a more open weave.

Sewing up

Mattress stitch

Place the pieces to be joined on a flat surface laid together side-by-side with right sides towards you. Using matching yarn, thread a needle back and forth with small, straight stitches. The stitches form a ladder between the two pieces of fabric, creating a flat, secure seam. This technique is usually known as mattress stitch.

Stocking stitch joins

The edges of stocking stitch tend to curl, so it may be tricky to join. The best way to join it is to use mattress stitch to pick up the bars between the columns of stitches.

Working upwards or downwards according to preference, secure the yarn to one of the pieces you want to join. Place the edges of the work together and pick up a bar from one side, then pick up the corresponding bar from the opposite side. Repeat.

After a few stitches, pull gently on the yarn and the two sides will come together in a seam that is almost invisible. Take care to stay in the same column all the way. Do not pull the stitches tight at first as you will not be able to see what you are doing.

Garter stitch joins

It is easier to join garter stitch as it has a firm edge and lies flat. Place the edges of the work together, right side up, and see where the stitches line up. Pick up the bottom loops of the stitches on one side of the work and the top loops of the stitches on the other side. After a few stitches, pull gently on the yarn. The stitches should lock together and lie completely flat. The inside of the join should look the same as it does on the outside.

Finishing touches

Backstitch

Work from right to left, bringing the needle up at point A, down at point B and then up at point C. Begin next stitch at point C. Repeat as required. Try to keep the distance between the stitches even.

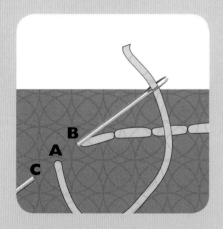

Pompoms

1 Cut out two cardboard circles a little smaller in diameter than the pompom you want. Make a hole in the middle of both about a third of the diameter. Put both circles together and using lengths of yarn, thread through the middle and begin wrapping around the outer edge until your card is completely covered. Use one or more colours for different effects. Continue working in this way until the centre hole is only a pinprick.

2 With sharp-ended scissors, cut all around the edge of the circle, slicing through all the strands of yarn.

3 Now ease a length of yarn between the card discs and tie very firmly around the centre, leaving a tail for sewing. You have now secured all the strands of yarn around the middle. Ease the card discs away from the pompom and fluff out all the strands. Trim off any loose or straggly ends.

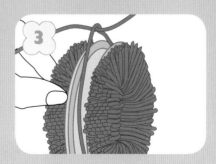

French knots

1 Bring needle to RS of fabric. Holding thread taut with finger and thumb of left hand, wind thread once or twice around needle tip.

2 Still holding thread, insert the needle tip close to the point where you brought the needle out to the RS of work and pull needle to back so that the twist lies neatly on the fabric surface. Repeat as required.

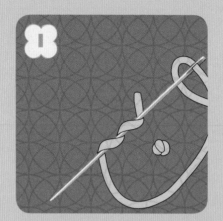

Making an I-cord

Using double-pointed needles, cast on the required number of sts – typically 5 sts. Do not turn work. Slide sts to the opposite end of the needle, then take the yarn firmly across the back of work. Knit sts again. Repeat to desired length. Cast off, or follow instructions in pattern.

Abbreviations

approx	approximately
beg	beginning
CC	contrast (colour)
ch	chain stitch
cm	centimetre
cont	continue
corresp	corresponding
dc	double crochet
dec	decrease
DK	double knitting
DPN(s)	double-pointed needles
foll	following
g-st	garter stitch
htr	half treble
in	inch
inc	increase by working twice into the stitch
K/k	knit
k-wise	knitwise, as if to knit
k1 tbl	knit 1 st through the back of the loop
k2tog	knit 2 sts together
LH	left-hand side

m	metre
MC	main (colour)
M1	make 1 stitch
M1L	make 1 stitch slanting left (left increase)
M1R	make 1 stitch slanting right (right increase)
mk	make
mm	millimetres
m-st	moss stitch
P/p	purl
patt	pattern
p2tog	purl two stitches together
psso	pass slipped stitch over
p-wise	purlwise, as if to purl
rem	remaining
rev st st	reverse stocking stitch
RS	right side of work
sk	skip
skpo	slip 1 st, k 1 st, pass slipped st over
sl	slip

sl-knot	slip knot
ss	slip stitch
ssk	slip 1 st k-wise, slip 1 st p-wise; knit these 2 sts together through the back of the loops
st(s)	stitch(es)
st st	stocking stitch
t-ch	turning chain
tog	together
tr	treble
trtr	triple treble
WS	wrong side of work
yb	yarn back
yd(s)	yard (s)
yf	yarn forward
yo	yarn over needle
wk	work
WS	wrong side of work
*	work instructions following *, then repeat as directed
( )	repeat instructions inside brackets as directed

Conversions

Knitting needle sizes

UK	Metric	US
12	2.75mm	2
11	3mm	–
10	3.25mm	3
–	3.5mm	4
9	3.75mm	5
8	4mm	6
7	4.5mm	7
6	5mm	8

Crochet hook sizes

UK	Metric	US
12	2.5mm	C/2
11	3mm	–
10	3.25mm	D/3
9	3.5mm	E/4
8	4mm	G/6
7	4.5mm	7
6	5mm	H/8

UK/US yarn weights

UK	US
2-ply	Lace
3-ply	Fingering
4-ply	Sport
Double knitting	Light worsted
Aran	Fisherman/worsted
Chunky	Bulky
Super chunky	Extra bulky

UK/US crochet terms

UK	US
Double crochet	Single crochet
Half treble	Half double crochet
Treble	Double crochet
Double treble	Triple crochet
Treble treble	Double triple crochet

Index

To place an order, or to request a catalogue, contact: **GMC Publications Ltd**
Castle Place, 166 High Street, Lewes, East Sussex, BN7 1XU, United Kingdom
Tel: +44 (0)1273 488005 **Fax:** +44 (0)1273 402866
www.gmcbooks.com

Egg Cozies